Crazy C

Also available in the Crazy activity series:

Crazy Cooking

Juliet Bawden

Designed by Jane Laycock
Illustrated by Jane Laycock
and Shelagh McGee

Beaver Books

A Beaver Book
Published by Arrow Books Limited
62–5 Chandos Place, London WC2N 4NW
An imprint of Century Hutchinson Ltd

London Melbourne Sydney Auckland
Johannesburg and agencies throughout the world

First published 1988

Set in Times by BookEns, Saffron Walden, Essex

Made and printed in Great Britain
by The Guernsey Press Co. Ltd.,
Guernsey, C.I.

ISBN 0 09 954330 3

For Douglas and Jacqueline Bullock

Contents

Before You Start

Yes I know it is rotten to have rules and regulations given to you just as you are about to have fun. However, kitchens can be very dangerous places if you are not careful! So always bear in mind the following points:

1. Always ask permission before you take over the kitchen, and make sure *you* wash and clear up as you go along – don't leave it all to your mum and dad!

2. Make sure your hands are clean and your nails scrubbed. Tie your hair back so it doesn't fall into the food.

3. Always read a recipe all the way through before starting to cook.

4. Both metric and imperial amounts have been given in these recipes. Stick to using only one system (e.g. *only* metric) as they are not exactly equal.

5. Make sure you have all the correct equipment and ingredients to hand before you start.

6. Always clear a space for putting down hot things and make sure there is a mat or something to put a hot plate or pan on to, so you don't burn yourself or the kitchen work tops.

7. Always pick up hot things with oven gloves or mitts.

8. If you do burn yourself, put the affected part under cold running water immediately and call for a parent or elder brother or sister to come and help.

9. Always wash fruit and vegetables before cooking them.

10. If you have younger brothers or sisters wandering about, make sure that any saucepan handles stick in towards the stove, and that knives and electric flexes do not hang over the edges of work tops.

11. Some of the recipes in this book use electrical equipment such as liquidizers and food mixers– these recipes are coded ● ● ● and should only be used when an adult is around to supervise. ● means the recipe is very easy and ● ● means it is a little more difficult. Remember that gas and electric cookers can be dangerous if not used correctly. Always have an adult with you when you are working at a cooker – and be particularly careful when you are lighting a gas stove.

12. *Never* touch electrical appliances with wet hands.

13. Have fun cooking!

Cooking Techniques

Aerating – Mixing air into ingredients to make a lighter mixture, for example, when making pastry (see page 125).

Beating – Mixing air into any semi-liquid mixture, such as eggs.

Breaking an egg – Cracking an egg so that the raw egg drops into a container while the eggshell remains in your hands.

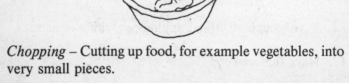

Chopping – Cutting up food, for example vegetables, into very small pieces.

Creaming – Beating fat or fat and sugar together until it is creamy both in texture and colour.

Curdle – If you add eggs too quickly to a mixture, the mixture might separate or 'curdle'. To prevent this, add a little flour with the eggs.

Dicing – Cutting up food, usually vegetables, into very small cubes.

Flaking – Breaking up fish with a fork, without chopping or crushing it.

Folding in – Mixing in very gently in a figure-of-eight movement to keep the air in the mixture.

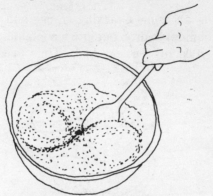

Garnishing – Decorating a dish to make it look appetizing, usually with something of a different colour and texture. It must be edible, for example, a few sprigs of parsley, a slice or two of lemon, or chopped hard-boiled eggs.

Greasing – Rubbing lard or other fat over the inside of a baking tin before adding the mixture to be cooked. This prevents the mixture sticking to the tin.

Kneading – Working and pressing dough or pastry with your hands.

Liquidizing – Mixing with liquid in an electric liquidizer until the food is a pulpy consistency.

Score – Slash with a sharp knife just through the surface.

Separating an egg – Cracking an egg and allowing the white (albumen) to drop out into a container, while keeping the yolk in the eggshell. This needs a bit of practice!

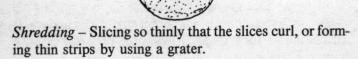

Shredding – Slicing so thinly that the slices curl, or forming thin strips by using a grater.

Sifting – Passing flour or icing sugar through a fine sieve to break up the lumps.

Stock – The liquid made from simmering bones, skin and scraps of meat in water to produce a broth or liquid for use in soups or stews. You can also make it by dissolving a stock cube in hot water.

Sweat – To cook food very gently in melted fat until it begins to give off or 'sweat' juice.

Whisking – Beating in air very rapidly, usually into egg whites.

Zest – The oil which gives the flavour to orange and lemon peel.

14

Finger Lickin' Chicken Dishes

There are a hundred and one ways to cook chicken. Here are just a few delicious ideas.

● Coronation Chicken

Serves 4
Time needed 25 mins

You will need

A cooked chicken about 1.25kg (3lb) in weight
325g (13oz) tin of curry sauce (Korma is a mild but spicy one, Rogan Josh is slightly hotter)
250ml (½pt) mayonnaise (see page 43)
125g (5oz) pot of natural yoghurt
Salt and pepper
Paprika

Equipment

Bowl
Tin opener
Wooden spoon

Instructions

1. Take the meat off the chicken bones and break it into largish chunks. Put it in a bowl.

2. Mix the tin of curry sauce, the mayonnaise and the natural yoghurt together with a wooden spoon and pour over the chicken.

3. Season with salt and pepper and then stir everything together well. Sprinkle with paprika before serving.

To serve:

Serve with rice or pitta bread and a green salad.

●●Chicken Pie

This is a good way of making a meal out of leftover chicken. If there isn't much chicken, use more mushrooms and onions.

Serves 5
Time needed 45 mins

You will need

1 large onion
100–200g (4–8oz) mushrooms
1 packet frozen puff pastry (defrosted)

Flour to roll out the pastry
Leftover cooked chicken
Salt and pepper

Equipment

Ovenproof pie dish with a lip
Tin opener
Rolling pin
Sharp knife
Chopping board
Fork

Instructions

1. Turn the oven on to 200°C/400°F/Gas Mark 6.

2. Peel and chop the onion and mushrooms finely, and put them in the pie dish.

3. Take the leftover chicken off the chicken carcass and rip it into bite-sized pieces. Add this to the pie dish.

4. Open the tin of soup and add to the pie dish. Season and stir well.

5. Roll the pastry out so that it is slightly bigger than the pie dish.

6. Cut off the extra pastry. Dampen the rim of the pie dish and put this extra pastry round the wet rim.

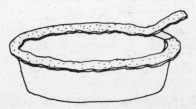

7. Put the rest of the pastry on top of the pie, pressing it down firmly on the pastry rim. Make a hole in the centre with a fork to let out steam.

8. Decorate the top with any leftover pastry cut into different shapes.

9. Put the pie in the oven and cook for about 30 minutes.

●● Chicken Casserole

This is a complete meal in one pot and is very easy to prepare. Make sure before you start cooking that your chicken is clean and there are no giblets inside! Frozen chickens should be completely thawed out before cooking.

Serves 5
Time needed: 20 min preparation plus 1½ hours cooking

18

You will need

6 small onions
4 fist-sized potatoes
2 carrots
1 small turnip
2 sticks of celery
1 parsnip
½ chicken stock cube
250ml (½pt) hot water
50g (2oz) butter
1.5kg (3lb 3oz) chicken
Salt and pepper

Equipment

Sharp knife
Chopping board
Large casserole dish

Instructions

1. Turn the oven on to 190°C/375°F/Gas Mark 5.

2. Peel and chop all the vegetables. Dissolve the stock cube in the hot water to make the chicken stock.

3. Melt the butter in the casserole.

4. Add the chicken and brown it on all sides.

5. Add the chopped vegetables, stock and seasoning. Cover with a lid or tin foil and place in the oven for 1½ hours until the chicken is tender.

To serve:

Serve with a green salad and bread.

Minced Meals

●● Beef Burgers

These are *real* beef burgers, not like the junk ones which are sold in some well-known burger bars!

Serves 4
Time needed 20 mins

You will need

400g (1lb) lean minced
   beef
1 small onion
Salt and pepper
Pinch of mixed herbs
1 egg

Equipment

Bowl
Sharp knife
Wooden spoon
Chopping board
Cup
Fork

Instructions

1. Put the mince in a bowl.

2. Peel and finely chop the onion. Add it to the mince and mix well.

3. Add a little salt and pepper, and the herbs.

4. Break the egg into a cup and beat it with a fork. Then add it to the mince mixture and mix well. The egg will bind the mixture together.

5. Divide the mixture up into eight portions, roll them into balls, and then flatten them with your hands into burger shapes.

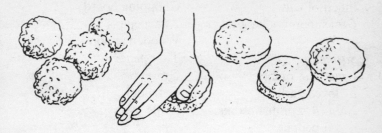

6. Cook under a grill, or fry them if you prefer, for 8 to 10 minutes. The thicker they are, the longer they will take to cook.

To serve:

Serve with buns, fried onions and tomato ketchup. It is also a good idea to put lots of sauces, mustards, cheese and salad on the table, so your guests can make up their own combinations.

●●● Spaghetti Bolognese

This meal does involve frying and using boiling water so be very careful!

Serves 4
Time needed 45 mins

21

You will need

200g (8oz) spaghetti
Pinch of salt
1 teaspoon cooking oil

Sauce:
1 medium onion
2 cloves garlic
100g (4oz) mushrooms
½ red pepper
2 tablespoons cooking oil
400g (1lb) lean minced beef
1 tablespoon tomato purée
200g (8oz) tin of tomatoes
1 bayleaf
Basil
Oregano
Salt and pepper
Lemon rind

Equipment

Sharp knife
Chopping board
2 saucepans
Wooden spoon
Tin opener
Grater
Colander
Ladle

Instructions

1. Make the sauce first. Peel the onion and garlic and chop them on a board.

2. Wash the mushrooms and wash and core the pepper, then chop them.

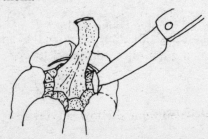

3. Put the oil in a saucepan and put it on a low heat. Add the chopped onions and garlic and cook until they look transparent, but not brown.

4. Add the meat to the onions and garlic and fry it until it turns brown.

5. Stir in the tomato purée with a wooden spoon.

6. Add the chopped red pepper and stir well.

7. Open the tin of tomatoes and add to the meat mixture.

8. Add the bayleaf, and a pinch of basil and oregano to the mixture.

9. Simmer for 25 minutes.

10. Add the chopped mushrooms and season with salt and pepper.

11. Grate a little lemon peel into the mixture, and simmer for a further 10 minutes.

12. Meanwhile, cook the spaghetti. Fill a large saucepan three-quarters full with water. Bring to the boil.

13. Add a pinch of salt and a teaspoon of cooking oil.

14. Add the spaghetti and stir. Cook it until it is firm, not soft (about 10 minutes). Remove a piece to test. It should be firm but not hard to bite.

15. Drain the spaghetti into the colander and stand it under the running hot tap to drain off the starch.

To serve:

1. Put the spaghetti in a shallow serving dish.

2. Carefully ladle the sauce into the centre of the spaghetti.

3. Serve the parmesan cheese, *or* grate cheddar cheese on the top and brown it under a hot grill!

Yummy!

●● Chilli con-Carne

This can be quite a hot dish so adjust your seasoning according to your taste, if you don't like hot food go very easy on the chilli powder.

Serves 4
Time needed 40 mins

You will need

500g (1lb) of minced beef
Oil to fry the onion
1 medium onion
1 clove of garlic
500g (1lb) tin of tomatoes
500g (1lb) tin of red
  kidney beans
½ red pepper
1 teaspoon cumin
1 teaspoon chilli powder
½ teaspoon cinnamon
1 bayleaf
2 cloves

Equipment

Chopping board
Sharp knife
Saucepan
Tin opener
Wooden spoon
Colander

Instructions

1. Peel and chop up garlic and onion.

2. Put a little oil in a saucepan and heat gently over a low heat. Add the chopped onions and garlic and cook gently without browning.

3. Add the meat and cook it until it browns.

4. Add all the spices, a little at a time. Stir well.

5. Add the can of tomatoes, stir well into the mixture, and simmer gently for 20 minutes.

6. Drain the kidney beans and throw away the juice. Add the beans to the meat and simmer for another 10 minutes.

7. Adjust the seasoning to taste.

To serve:

Serve with rice, garlic bread and a green salad.

Vegetable Savouries

●● Spicy Vegetable Soup

This soup is delicious and very filling.

Serves 6
Time needed 40 mins

You will need

3 carrots
4 small potatoes
1 pepper
200g (8oz) mushrooms
3 medium onions
1 clove garlic
2 tablespoons cooking oil
1 tablespoon tomato purée
1 vegetable stock cube
1 pint hot water
1 200g (8oz) tin of tomatoes
Pinch of mixed herbs
1 teaspoon chilli powder
½ teaspoon cumin

Equipment

Sharp knife
Chopping board

Large saucepan with lid
Wooden spoon
Tin opener

Instructions

1. Peel the carrots and potatoes.

2. Wash and core the pepper, and wash the mushrooms. Dice them.

3. Peel the onion and garlic and chop them.

4. Heat the oil in a large saucepan on a low heat and add the chopped onions and garlic. Cover with a lid. Cook until the onions begin to look transparent, but not brown.

5. Add the tomato purée and stir well.

6. Make the vegetable stock, by dissolving the stock cube in a pint of hot water. Add this to the saucepan.

7. Add the tin of tomatoes to the saucepan. Bring to the boil.

8. Add the chopped carrots and potatoes to the pan, and simmer for half an hour.

9. Keep checking to make sure there is enough liquid in the pan. If it looks like it is drying up, add some more vegetable stock or water.

10. When the carrots and potatoes are fairly soft, add the chopped pepper and simmer for another 10 minutes.

11. Then add the chopped mushrooms.

12. Add the mixed herbs, chilli powder, and cumin. Stir well and serve hot.

To serve:

Serve with lots of warm crusty bread. If you like, grate some cheddar cheese over the soup.

●● Ratatouille

This recipe is nothing to do with rats! In fact, it is a very good dish to serve to a vegetarian.

Serves 6
Time needed 1 hour 15 mins

You will need

2 medium-sized onions
2 cloves of garlic
1 red pepper
1 green pepper
400g (1lb) aubergines
400g (1lb) mushrooms
400g (1lb) courgettes
2 400g (1lb) tins of
    tomatoes
3 tablespoons olive oil
Pinch mixed herbs
Salt and pepper

Equipment

Sharp knife
Chopping board
Tin opener
Large saucepan
Wooden spoon

Instructions

1. Peel and roughly chop the onions and garlic.

2. Dice the peppers and the aubergines, chop the mushrooms, and slice the courgettes.

3. Open the tins of tomatoes.

4. Heat the olive oil in a large saucepan and add the onions, garlic and mixed herbs.

5. Add the chopped aubergines, peppers, mushrooms and courgettes.

6. Cook for about five minutes, stirring with a wooden spoon.

7. Add the tomatoes and enough water to cover the vegetables.

8. Simmer for 1 hour.

9. Season with salt and pepper before serving.

To serve:

Serve with baked potatoes or freshly made bread rolls for a main course. Or serve it as a vegetable dish with chicken.

●●● Hummus

This dish is Middle Eastern in origin, and is usually eaten with pitta bread.

Serves 6
Time needed 25 mins

You will need

400g (1lb) tin of chick peas
Juice of 1 lemon
1 clove of garlic
3–4 tablespoons olive oil
3–4 tablespoons tahini paste (you can buy this in health
    food shops – it looks and tastes a bit like pale
    peanut butter)
Salt and pepper
Mint leaves for decoration

Equipment

Tin opener
Colander
Bowl
Fork
Electric liquidizer (useful but not essential)
Garlic press
Wooden spoon

Instructions

1. Empty the tin of chick peas into the colander and rinse well under the cold tap.

2. Then put them into a bowl and add the lemon juice. Mash together with a fork. (*Or* mix them in a liquidizer.)

3. Peel the garlic, crush it in the garlic press, and then add to the mixture.

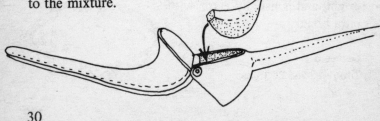

4. Stir in the olive oil and tahini paste with a wooden spoon. The hummus should be the consistency of mayonnaise. If it is too thick, add more oil.

5. Season with salt and pepper and decorate with mint leaves.

Food Parcels

Parcels are always good fun to open, especially ones containing food! You can have sweet or savoury food parcels and there are lots of different combinations – mince pies, for instance, are delicious Christmas food parcels, while pitta bread stuffed with cheese and ham makes a tasty savoury parcel. Why not experiment and invent your own!

●●● Stuffed Pepper Parcels

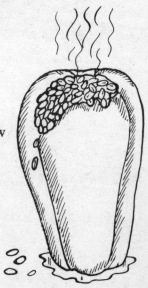

Serves 4
Time needed 1 hour 15 mins

You will need

4 peppers – red, green or yellow
Salt
Little olive oil

Stuffing:

200g (8oz) rice
4 small onions
200g (8oz) chopped nuts
200g (8oz) seedless raisins

Pinch of oregano
Salt and pepper

Equipment

2 saucepans
Colander
2 sharp knives
Chopping board
Bowl
Wooden spoon
Spoon
Pastry brush
Ovenproof dish and lid or foil

Instructions

1. First prepare the stuffing. Cook the rice in a saucepan of boiling water until it is quite soft and sticky (about 15 minutes). Drain it in a colander.

2. Peel and chop the onions and mix them with the rice in a bowl. Add the chopped nuts and mix well.

3. Chop the raisins and add to the same mixture.

4. Season the mixture with oregano, salt and pepper. Set on one side while you prepare the peppers.

5. Turn the oven on to 160°C/325°F/Gas Mark 3.

6. Boil a pan of water with a little salt in, and then plunge the peppers into it for 1 minute.

7. Carefully remove the peppers and leave them to cool.

8. With a sharp knife cut around the base of the stalk (see the diagram on page 34).

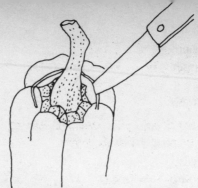

9. Remove the stalk, the core and the seeds, leaving you with a gap in the top of your pepper through which to put the filling. Repeat for each pepper.

10. Spoon the stuffing mixture into each pepper through the gap in the top.

11. Brush the outside of the peppers with olive oil and pack them tightly in an ovenproof dish.

12. Cover the dish with foil, or a lid if it has one, and bake in the oven for about 40–45 minutes or until the peppers are soft.

Ideas

Use the same stuffing mixture to stuff other vegetables, such as tomatoes, onions or marrows.

●●● Cheese Puff

This is a good dish to serve with salad for lunch. It is an easy version of a Greek cheese pie.

Serves 5
Time needed 45 mins

You will need

500g (1lb 4oz) bought puff pastry (if it is frozen take it out
  in plenty of time for it to thaw)
1 egg
100g (4oz) cheddar cheese
Salt and pepper
150g (6oz) cottage cheese
Flour for rolling out

Equipment

Rolling pin
Bowl
Fork
Grater
Wooden spoon
Sharp knife
Baking tray

Instructions

1. Turn the oven on at 200°C/400°F/Gas Mark 6.

2. Sprinkle some flour on a clean, flat surface, and on top
of it roll out the pastry into an oblong as thin as you can
make it without making holes in it.

3. Break the egg into a bowl and beat it with a fork.

4. Grate the cheddar cheese into the same bowl and then
add the salt and pepper.

5. Mix in the cottage cheese with a wooden spoon.

6. Spread the mixture on the centre of your pastry oblong.

7. Fold in the two sides of the pastry to the centre and overlap them. Then turn up the bottom and top edges of the pastry, so the mixture doesn't seep out.

8. Very gently flatten the cheese puff with a rolling pin and with a sharp knife score sections down it.

9. Lift the cheese puff on to a baking tray and cook in the oven for approximately 30 minutes. It will puff up and look spectacular.

To serve:

Serve with a green salad for lunch or supper.

36

●● Stuffed Apple Dumplings

Serves 4
Time needed 50 mins

You will need

1 lemon
4 large eating apples or cooking apples of the same
  size.
500g (1lb 4oz) pastry (you can buy this ready-made, or
  make your own, see page 125)
1 egg
A little margarine (for greasing baking tray)

Filling

A mixture of any of the following: brown sugar, grated
lemon rind, mincemeat, chopped dates, raisins, honey and
chopped nuts

Equipment

Lemon squeezer
Apple corer
Sharp knife
Pastry brush
Rolling pin
Cup
Fork
Baking tray

Instructions

1. Turn the oven on to 190°/375°F/Gas Mark 5.

2. Squeeze the lemon and keep the juice on one side.

3. Using the corer, remove the centre from each of the four apples.

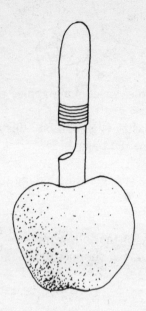

4. Peel the apples and brush with lemon juice to prevent them from turning brown.

5. Divide the pastry evenly into four pieces and roll each piece into a square approximately 20cm × 20cm (8ins × 8ins).

6. Fill the apples with your mixture and place each apple in the centre of a pastry square.

7. Break the egg into a cup and beat it with a fork.

8. Brush each edge of the pastry square with beaten egg and bring the four corners of the square up to the top of the apple. Pinch them together to seal the pastry case.

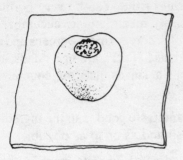

9. Cut out leaf shapes from any bits of leftover pastry. Dip them in the beaten egg and then stick them on the top of the apples for decoration.

10. Grease a baking tray and place the wrapped apples on it.

11. Brush the pastry-covered apples with beaten egg, and then cook for 35 minutes.

Super Salads

Salads can be wonderful or they can be very boring. A salad does not necessarily mean lettuce, cucumber and tomato – there are lots of different kinds of greens and non-greens to use as your basis. There are egg salads, meat salads, fish salads, pasta salads and, of course, fruit salads.

Salads should look and taste good, and the ingredients must always be as fresh and as crisp as possible.

You can make a salad as a complete meal in itself, a starter, or a side dish to serve with other food.

● Quick 'n' Easy Salad Ideas

3 bean salad

Open a tin of each of the following – red kidney beans, green flageolets, and butter beans – and drain away the liquid. Pile all the beans together on a bed of lettuce and serve.

Carrot and raisin salad

Mix 400g (1lb) grated carrots with 100g (4oz) raisins and toss them together in 2 tablespoons of soy sauce.

Tomato salad

Cut 400g (1lb) tomatoes into slices, and 1 onion into rings. Serve them together with 2 tablespoons of olive oil and a sprinkling of chopped parsley.

Coleslaw

Clean and grate 250g (10oz) white cabbage and 125g (5oz) carrots. Mix them together with 50g (2oz) unsalted peanuts and 50g (2oz) raisins. Dress with a 125g (5oz) pot of yoghurt mixed with 125g (5oz) mayonnaise.

● Speedy Potato Salad

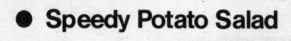

Serves 4
Time needed 15 mins

You will need

500g (1lb) Tin of potatoes
100g (4oz) mayonnaise
  (page 43)
A bunch of chives

Equipment

Tin opener
Sharp knife
Chopping board
Shallow dish
Wooden spoon
Kitchen scissors

Instructions

1. Open the tin of potatoes and drain away the liquid.

2. Chop the potatoes into cubes approximately 1cm square.

3. Put the potatoes in a dish and then add the mayonnaise. Mix together well, so that the potatoes are coated with the mayonnaise.

4. Wash the chives and shake dry.

5. Using kitchen scissors, chop up the chives into 5mm pieces and sprinkle them on top of the potatoes.

●● Chicken Salad

Serves 5
Time needed 30 mins

You will need

500g (1lb 4oz) pasta spirals
1 medium cold roasted chicken
1 small onion or a bunch of spring onions
Few sprigs of fresh mint
125g (5oz) pot of natural yoghurt
Salt and pepper

Equipment

Saucepan
Colander
Bowl
Sharp knife
Chopping board
Wooden spoon

Instructions

1. Cook the pasta spirals in a saucepan of boiling water for 10 minutes. Then drain in the colander and leave to cool.

2. Take the meat off the chicken bones and break it into bite-sized pieces. Put it in a bowl.

3. Chop the onions or spring onions finely, and add to the chicken.

4. Add the pasta spirals.

5. Chop the mint and add to the mixture.

6. Then add the yoghurt, and season with salt and pepper. Mix everything together with a wooden spoon.

●●● Easy Mayonnaise

GLURP!

Makes 125ml (¼pt)
Time needed 5 mins

You will need

1 egg
1–2 tablespoons vinegar
1 teaspoon french mustard
¼ teaspoon salt
A little pepper
1 teaspoon sugar
125ml (¼pt) sunflower
   seed oil

Equipment

Liquidizer
Bowl *or* screw-topped jar

Instructions

1. Break the egg into the liquidizer and whizz for 30 seconds.

2. Add the vinegar, mustard, salt, pepper and sugar, and whizz for another 10 seconds.

3. With the liquidizer on as slow as possible, gradually pour the oil into the mixture until the mayonnaise becomes thick and glossy. It is now ready to use, or if you like you can store it in a screw-topped jar in the fridge.

● **Vinaigrette Dressing**

This is lovely dressing for any sort of salad, and much cheaper to make than to buy! It is also delicious in the centre of a cut avocado or poured over a tomato salad (see page 41). When made, keep it in a jar in the fridge, so you have some whenever you make a salad.

Time needed 5 mins

You will need

1 clove of garlic
2 heaped teaspoons honey
1 heaped teaspoon
  mustard powder
Pepper (freshly ground
  if possible)
2 tablespoons wine vinegar
6 tablespoons olive oil

Equipment

Sharp knife
Garlic press
Fork
Plate
Clean jam jar with lid
Teaspoon

Instructions

1. Peel the clove of garlic and crush it in a garlic press or mash it with a fork on a plate (so you don't lose the juice) and then chop it finely.

2. Put the garlic in the jam jar with the honey, mustard powder and pepper to taste, and stir it all together with a teaspoon.

3. Add the vinegar and the oil, put the lid on the jar and shake it thoroughly to blend all the ingredients. Always remember to shake the jar well before using the vinaigrette.

Ideas

Use lemon juice instead of vinegar. Or use chopped mint instead of garlic.

Cheats' Corner

This section isn't so much about cheating as saving time and cutting corners. You can make very good dishes using a combination of convenience foods and fresh foods.

● Tomato Soup

Serves 4
Time needed 5 mins

You will need

200g (8oz) tin of tomato
  soup
200g (8oz) tin of tomatoes
Sprig of fresh parsley
Salt and pepper

Equipment

Tin opener
Saucepan
Wooden spoon
Sharp knife
Chopping board

Instructions

1. Open the soup and the tomatoes, and pour them both into a saucepan.

2. Heat the mixture on a low heat, stirring all the time.

3. Chop the parsley finely.

4. Season the soup with salt and pepper. Just before serving, sprinkle the chopped parsley on top.

Ideas

Pour a swirl of single cream, or the top from some full fat milk, on the soup before serving it. Buy ready-made croutons and serve with the soup or serve crisps for an unusual accompaniment.

●● Cheats' French Onion Soup

Serves 4
Time needed 15 mins

You will need

2 200g (8oz) tins of French onion soup
1 tablespoon brandy or sherry (with your parents' permission!)
1 loaf of French bread
50g (2oz) cheddar cheese

Equipment

Tin opener
Saucepan
Wooden spoon
Bread knife
Grater

Instructions

1. Empty the tins of soup into a saucepan and put it on a low heat.

2. When the soup is hot, add the brandy or sherry, and stir well.

3. Cut the French bread into slices about 2cm thick.

4. Grate the cheese on to the top of each piece of French bread.

5. Serve each bowl of soup with a piece of French bread and cheese floating on top.

●● Easy Bread Rolls

Crisp white rolls straight from the oven. What could be more delicious?

Makes 1 small loaf or about 8 rolls
Time needed 1 hour 45 mins (loaf) *or* **1 hour 15 mins (rolls)**

You will need

1 500g (1lb 4oz) packet of white bread dough mixture containing active yeast (obtainable at most supermarkets)

Equipment

Bowl
Baking tray
Damp cloth or greased polythene bag

Instructions

1. Prepare the dough mixture, following the instructions on the pack.

2. Divide the dough into fist-sized pieces. Roll one into a sausage shape and then twist it round to make a circle or a letter 'S'. Or plait three sausage-shaped pieces of dough together to make a plaited loaf. To make a cottage loaf, take two balls of dough, one larger than the other. Put the smaller one on top of the larger one and push a finger through the centre to make a dimple.

3. Place the dough rolls on a baking tray.

4. Cover them with a damp cloth or plastic bag.

5. Leave in a warm place for 35–40 minutes, or until the dough has nearly doubled in size.

6. Whilst the bread is rising, preheat the oven to 230°C/450°F/Gas Mark 8.

7. Bake the rolls in the oven; a cottage loaf takes approximately 40–45 minutes to cook, while the bread rolls take about 10–15 minutes.

● Ice Cream Dreams

Here are a number of suggestions for cheering up a bowl of boring old ice cream.

1. Sprinkle some flaked almonds on a piece of tin foil and put this under the grill until they turn brown. Then sprinkle them on on top of ice cream.

2. For sophisticated adult tastes, melt plain chocolate ice cream and pour this over vanilla ice cream. Stick either peppermint or orange sticks all over the top.

3. Melt 100g (4oz) plain chocolate in a bowl over hot water and add 1 teaspoon of coffee granules dissolved in 1 teaspoon of water. Stir the mixture well, and then pour over ice cream.

4. Add any combination of tinned or fresh fruit and top that with squirty cream.

● Chocolate Sauce

This is a delicious sauce, especially when poured over ice cream.

Serves 4
Time needed 15 mins

You will need

3 tablespoons milk
3 Milky Ways

Equipment

Saucepan
Wooden spoon

Instructions

1. Put the milk in a saucepan and warm it over a low heat. Do not let it boil.

2. Break up the Milky Ways into small pieces, and add them to the milk.

3. Stir the mixture with a wooden spoon over a low heat until the chocolate melts and the sauce is thick and smooth.

To serve:

Pour the sauce while still hot over ice cream.

Making Faces

You can turn almost any kind of food, sweet or savoury, into a face. Biscuits are good for this purpose, as they are usually round, like a face. But you can also make faces from baked potatoes, pizzas, bread rolls, cake and fruit.

● Savoury Biscuit Faces

There are many ingredients listed below, but you do not need all of them. Remember that you are going to eat these, so choose the ingredients that you like. Also try to choose food with different colours so that the faces look interesting!

Time needed about 30 mins

You will need

Biscuit bases:

Water biscuits
Cream crackers
Ritz biscuits

Face decorations:

Salami

Equipment

Knife
Grater

Carrots
Red and green peppers
Cucumber
Cheddar cheese
Cottage cheese
Miniature gherkins
Raisins
Tomato
Olives
Sweetcorn
Cheese spread or butter or table margarine
Marmite or Bovril
Anchovies

Instructions

1. Spread some of your biscuits with cream cheese or butter. If you would like some brown or black faces, mix the spread, butter or cream cheese with marmite or bovril. Leave other biscuits bare and use one of the spreads to stick the features on to the biscuits.

2. Cut the circular ingredients for eyes, such as gherkins, olives, baby carrots and cocktail onions.

3. To make the hair, grate carrot or cheese or cut the salami into strips. Or you could use tomatoes, cucumber, sweetcorn, or green or red peppers.

4. Make a nose, mouth and eyebrows out of other ingredients. Make some faces sad, others happy, and give them all different characteristics – add beards of cottage cheese, an anchovy moustache, or large cucumber ears. Just experiment and have fun!

● Sweet Biscuit Faces

These are similar to the savoury
biscuits, but instead of using
savoury toppings, you use sweet
ones, or a combination of the two.

Time needed about 30 mins

You will need

Biscuit bases:

Coconut biscuits for a bumpy face
Chocolate biscuits for a brown face
Digestives

Face decorations:

Plain icing (page 87)
Liquorice strips
Small sweets such as liquorice allsorts
Jelly sweets
Smarties
Hundreds and thousands
Glace**A** cherries, angelica, silver balls and other cake
    decorations
Chocolate drops

Instructions

Make as for savoury biscuit faces. Use icing to stick the
sweets on with, and experiment using as many different
sweets and decorations as you can think of.

●●● Yoghurt Pizza Face

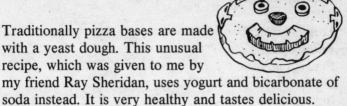

Traditionally pizza bases are made with a yeast dough. This unusual recipe, which was given to me by my friend Ray Sheridan, uses yogurt and bicarbonate of soda instead. It is very healthy and tastes delicious.

Time needed 30 mins

You will need

100g (4oz) wholemeal flour
1 teaspoon bicarbonate of soda
1 teaspoon cream of tartar
4 tablespoons plain yoghurt
2 tablespoons olive oil

Sauce:

1 small onion
1 clove of garlic
50g (2oz) mushrooms
1 tablespoon olive oil
200g (8oz) tin of tomatoes
Oregano
150g (6oz) grated cheese

Optional extras:

Chopped anchovies, olives, ham, pineapple, salami

Equipment

Sharp knife

Chopping board
Saucepan
Wooden spoon
Tin opener
Large bowl
Rolling pin
Frying pan

Instructions

1. First prepare the sauce. Peel and chop the onion finely, and peel and crush the garlic.

2. Clean and slice the mushrooms.

3. Pour the olive oil in the saucepan, heat it over a low heat, and gently fry the onions, garlic and mushrooms.

4. Stir in the tomatoes and juice, and a sprinkle of oregano, and cook for a little while longer.

5. Meanwhile, make the pizza base. Mix together in the bowl the flour, the bicarbonate of soda and the cream of tartar.

6. Add the yoghurt and mix well until the mixture forms a large ball.

7. Dust the table or work top with flour and roll out the dough into a circle slightly smaller than the frying pan you are about to use.

8. Heat the oil in the pan.

9. Add the circle of dough and fry it gently until it turns golden brown on one side. Then turn it over and fry the other side. (The dough will also rise.)

10. Take it off the heat and then add the topping.

11. Grate the cheese over the pizza base.

12. Spoon over the sauce you have just made.

13. Decorate the top of the pizza with any combination of the optional extras, so that it looks like a face. Use anchovies for eyebrows, olives for eyes and half a pineapple ring for a mouth, for example.

14. Place under a hot grill until the topping bubbles.

Ideas

If you don't have time to make a pizza base, use toast, crumpets, muffins or slices of French bread instead.

●● Baked Potato Faces

Baked potatoes are delicious, very nutritious and can make a complete meal on their own.

tomato slices

pickled onion

gherkin

cucumber

Serves 2
Time needed 1 hour 15 mins

You will need

2 large potatoes of equal size
Butter (optional)

Filling:

1 175g (7oz) tin of tuna
2 avocados

Equipment

Brush
Kitchen paper
Fork
Baking tray (optional)
Oven gloves
Skewer
Bowl

Potato masher
Tin opener
Sharp knife
Spoon

8 tablespoons cottage
  cheese
Salt and pepper
Lemon juice

Instructions

1. Turn the oven on to 200°C/400°F/Gas Mark 6.

2. Scrub the potatoes very well with a brush – a nail brush is quite good for this.

3. Pat the potatoes dry with kitchen paper.

4. Prick each potato all over with a fork. (This will stop them exploding in the oven!)

5. If you wish you can rub the potatoes over with butter to keep the skins soft.

6. Place the potatoes either on the open shelves of the oven, or on a baking tray.

7. Cook for 1–1½ hours.

8. To test to see if they are cooked, first put on oven gloves so you don't burn yourself removing the potatoes from the oven. Prick the potatoes with a skewer. If the skewer goes in easily, the potatoes are ready.

9. Cut each potato in half and scoop out most of the flesh into a bowl, leaving the skin whole.

10. Mash the cooked potato flesh with a masher or fork until light and fluffy. Put it to one side.

11. Strain the oil or brine from the tin of tuna.

12. Flake the tuna into the potato mixture and mix well.

13. Peel the avocados and then cut them into cubes and add to the mixture.

14. Add the cottage cheese and stir.

15. Season with salt, pepper and a little lemon juice.

16. Pile the mixture back in the potato skins and put into the oven for another 5 minutes before serving.

17. You can turn the filling into a face – see *Ideas*.

Other fillings

The method for making these fillings is the same as above – chop all ingredients and mix together with the cooked mashed potato. Each filling serves 2.

1. 2 mushrooms, 6 thick slices of cucumber and 6 table-spoons of mayonnaise.

2. 4 slices of ham, 125g (5oz) carton of sour cream or yoghurt, 4 teaspoons of chives or spring onion stems.

3. 4 tablespoons of grated cheddar cheese and 2 dessert-spoons of chutney.

Ideas

Make up your own fillings and turn them into faces in the same way as you did with the biscuits. Use cocktail sticks to stick pieces of cucumber, carrot, hard-boiled eggs, gherkins, or olives on to the potato to make eyes.

Stick one half of the potato on top of the other and fill the opening at the front with sweetcorn for teeth.

Cut out a long red tongue from a red pepper.

Make hair from mustard and cress, parsley or chives.

Quirky Combinations

●●● Orange, Carrot and Tomato Soup

Serves 6
Time needed 1½ hours

You will need

200g (8oz) onions
2 cloves of garlic
1 tablespoon cooking oil
400g (1lb) carrots
1 400g (1lb) tin of
    tomatoes
2 large oranges
Tomato purée
Little water
1 bay leaf
Pinch of oregano
Salt and pepper

Equipment

Saucepan
Sharp knife
Chopping board
Tin opener
Grater
Lemon squeezer
Sieve or liquidizer

Instructions

1. Peel and chop the onions and garlic.

2. Put the oil in a saucepan and heat it over a low heat.

Add the onion and garlic and cook gently.

3. Peel and chop the carrots.

4. Add the carrots to the saucepan.

5. Open the tin of tomatoes and add to the saucepan.

6. Simmer the vegetables gently for 5 minutes.

7. Using a fine grater, grate *some* of the orange peel into the saucepan.

8. Cut the oranges in half and squeeze the juice in a lemon squeezer. Add this to the saucepan.

9. Add a little tomato purée and water to the soup. Then add the bay leaf and a pinch of oregano.

10. Simmer the soup for an hour, making sure that it doesn't get too thick. If it does, add more water.

11. Take the saucepan off the heat, allow the soup to cool and either sieve it or blend it in a liquidizer.

12. Season with salt and pepper to taste.

To serve:

Serve the soup either hot or cold, with lots of crusty bread rolls.

●●● Apple Curry Soup

Serves 5
Time needed 1 hour

You will need

2 chicken or vegetable stock cubes
1000ml (2pts) boiling water
2 medium onions
1 large cooking apple
2 tablespoons cooking oil
2 teaspoons curry powder or curry paste
2 tablespoons plain yoghurt
Salt and pepper

Equipment

Sharp knife
Chopping board
Saucepan
Liquidizer or sieve
Bowl (to rest sieve on)
Wooden spoon

Instructions

1. Dissolve the stock cubes in the boiling water.

2. Peel and chop the onions and cooking apple.

3. Heat the oil in a saucepan and then add the chopped onions. Fry them over a low heat until they are transparent.

4. Add the curry powder or paste.

5. Add the chopped apple and the stock, and bring back to the boil. Simmer for 20–30 minutes.

6. Leave the soup to cool for 15 minutes.

7. Then, either strain the soup through a sieve, or purée in the liquidizer.

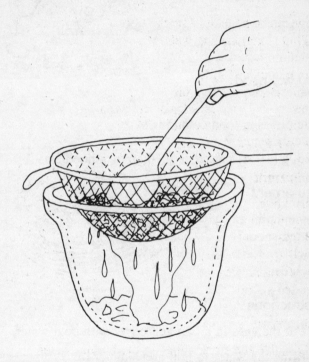

8. Add the yoghurt, then the salt and pepper, and stir well.

9. Return the soup to the saucepan and reheat, but do not boil or the soup will separate.

●● Marbled Eggs in a Nest of Noodles

These eggs look very pretty, especially if you serve them on a bed of egg noodles arranged to look like a bird's nest.

Serves 6
Time needed 30 mins

You will need

6 eggs
Blue or green food colouring
Ice cubes
1 250g (10oz) packet of medium egg noodles

Equipment

Saucepan
Slotted spoon
Bowl
Colander

Instructions

1. Put the eggs in a pan and cover with cold water.

2. Bring the water to boil and simmer for 3 minutes.

3. Very carefully remove the eggs from the water using a slotted spoon.

4. Add 2 teaspoons of food colouring to the water so it becomes quite dark.

5. Tap the eggs all over with the back of a spoon so that the shells crack and look like crazy paving.

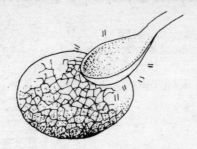

6. Return the eggs to the water and cook for a further 6 minutes.

7. Fill a bowl with cold water and add 3 or 4 ice cubes and a teaspoonful of food colouring.

8. Plunge the eggs into the coloured iced water and leave for 10 minutes. Meanwhile, cook the egg noodles.

9. Bring a large saucepan of water to the boil.

10. Drop the noodles into the water and then remove the pan from the heat.

11. Leave the noodles in the water for 6 minutes, and then strain them through a colander.

12. Remove the eggs from the iced water, and take off their shells to reveal marbled eggs.

13. Arrange the noodles as a nest in a large bowl and put the eggs in the middle.

Idea

Use spaghetti instead of noodles.

●●● Cheese and Mustard Bread and Butter Pudding

This is an unusual supper dish which is based on bread and butter pudding, but is savoury rather than sweet.

Serves 4
Time needed 1 hour 10 mins

You will need

12 slices of brown bread
Butter or margarine to spread on them
200–300g (8–12oz) cheese, depending on how cheesey you like your food! Use cheddar, stilton or any leftover cheese.
800ml (1½pts) milk
4 eggs
2 teaspoons coarse mustard (optional)
Salt and pepper

Equipment

Shallow ovenproof dish
Sharp knife
Grater
Bowl

Instructions

1. Turn the oven on to 200°C/400°F/Gas Mark 6.

2. Grease the ovenproof dish.

3. Cut the crusts off the bread. (You could feed them to the birds, or to ducks in the park.) Butter the slices of bread quite thickly.

4. Cut the bread into quarters, and put a layer in the dish, butter side up, to cover the bottom and sides of the dish.

5. Grate half the cheese over this layer.

6. Put in another layer of bread, butter side up, and grate the rest of the cheese over the top.

7. If there is any bread left, put this on top of the cheese, butter side up.

8. Mix together the milk, eggs, mustard, salt and pepper in a bowl.

9. Pour this mixture over the bread pudding.

10. Bake in the oven for 50 minutes.

To serve:

Serve piping hot with a crisp, green salad.

Crazy Cakes

Before you make any of the cakes in this book read this page first! Cake making can be easy provided you follow a few simple rules:

1. Unless the recipe says otherwise, turn your oven on before you start so that it is at the correct temperature by the time you come to put the cake in.

2. If the cake recipe contains fat (butter or margarine), make sure that it is at room temperature before you start using it. If the fat is straight from the fridge, it will be cold and hard and impossible to mix.

3. Always sieve flour and other dry ingredients before mixing them. This gets rid of lumps and adds extra air, making the finished cake lighter.

4. It is easy to curdle a cake mixture when adding eggs too quickly. This means that the mixture separates and won't mix smoothly. If you cook a cake that has curdled, it won't rise as high as one that didn't curdle. To prevent this, beat the eggs in a bowl and add a little at a time, with a small amount of the flour, to your creamed sugar and fat.

5. Always grease your cake tins to prevent the cake sticking. If the cake is a heavy one, such as a rich fruit cake, it is a good idea to line the cake tin with greaseproof paper as well (see the diagram on page 70).

●●● Victoria Sponge

This is the basic recipe for a
sponge cake. You can alter it as
you wish by adding different
flavourings. Once you have mastered this recipe, you will
be able to go on and try a novelty Victoria sponge (see
page 69).

Serves 6–8
Time needed 40 minutes

You will need

100g (4oz) butter
100g (4oz) caster sugar
2 eggs
100g (4oz) self-raising
flour
A little margarine (for
greasing tins)

Filling:

Butter icing *or*
Jam and cream

Equipment

2 20cm cake tins
Greaseproof paper (for
lining tins)
Mixing bowl
Wooden spoon
Food mixer (optional)
Cup
Fork
Sieve
Bowl

Instructions

1. Turn the oven on to 180°C/350°F/Gas Mark 4.

2. Grease and line two 20cm cake tins (see diagram on
page 70).

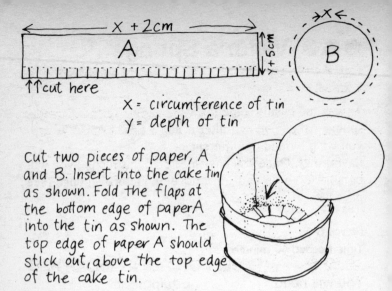

x = circumference of tin
y = depth of tin

Cut two pieces of paper, A and B. Insert into the cake tin as shown. Fold the flaps at the bottom edge of paper A into the tin as shown. The top edge of paper A should stick out, above the top edge of the cake tin.

3. Cream the butter and sugar together in a large mixing bowl with a wooden spoon. If you prefer, you can use a food mixer. From time to time you will need to scrape the mixture from the sides of the bowl. Continue mixing until the mixure is light and fluffy.

4. Break the eggs into a cup and beat with a fork.

5. Sift the flour into another bowl.

6. Gradually add the eggs to the creamed butter and sugar. At the same time add a small amount of sifted flour to stop the mixture curdling (separating).

7. Add half the remaining flour to the mixture and mix well, then fold in the rest.

8. Divide the mixture evenly between the two cake tins and bake in the oven for 20–25 minutes.

9. When the two cakes are cool, sandwich them together with butter icing (see page 86) or with jam and cream.

Ideas

Vary the flavour of your cake by adding or substituting different ingredients:

Cocoa: Replace 25g (1oz) flour with 25g (1oz) cocoa powder. If the mixture is dry, add a little orange juice.

Coffee: Mix a teaspoon of coffee powder or granules with a very small amount of water and add to the cake mixture with the flour. Add a few chopped walnuts for extra crunch.

●●● Novelty Victoria Sponge

To make a novelty cake which will be heavily decorated or built up in slabs, you need a heavier mixture than the basic Victoria sponge. Use 150g (6oz) self-raising flour instead of 100g (4oz). With this basic recipe and lots of imagination you can make a cake fit for any occasion.

For example, use circular cake tins to make heads, clocks and numbers such as 3, 6 and 8. Use square or oblong cake tins for making cars or houses. You can even bake a cake in a pudding basin if you want the shape of a ladybird, tortoise, a crinoline dress or an igloo, for instance. Other cakes can be made from a combination of different shapes, cut and stuck together with jam.

Serves 8
Time needed 1½ hours including decoration

You will need

100g (4 oz) butter
100g (4oz) caster sugar
2 eggs
150g (6oz) self-raising flour
Jam
A little margarine (for greasing tins)

Icing:

Plain icing (page 87) *or* butter icing (page 86) *or* fondant
  icing (page 85)

Decoration:

Any of the following:
Food colouring
Chocolate drops
Small sweets and biscuits
Glacé cherries
Liquorice
Cocktail sticks
Cocktail umbrellas
Hundreds and thousands
Desiccated coconut
Wafers and ice cream cones

Equipment

Cake tins
Greaseproof paper (for lining tins)
Mixing bowl
Wooden spoon
Food mixer (optional)
Cup

Fork
Sieve
Bowl
Double saucepan or bowl which fits into a saucepan

Instructions

1. Follow the instructions for making a Victoria sponge. The cake tins you use will depend on what sort of novelty cake you want.

2. Once the cake is cooked and left to cool, build it into the shape you want by cutting out shapes and sticking them together with jam.

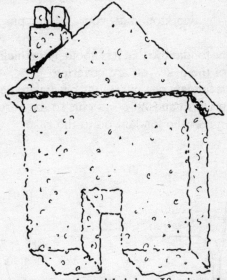

3. Then cover your cake with icing. If using **plain icing**, you will have to spread it on quickly with a knife, before it begins to harden. **Butter icing** is easier to spread on, and you can make it look choppy or smooth. **Fondant icing** takes longer as it needs a jam glaze to glue it to the cake.

Jam Glaze

Fill the saucepan or the lower saucepan if using a double one, with very hot water. Put the jam into the top saucepan or bowl. Stir until it melts and goes runny. Then spread it over the cake. This works like glue and will stick the icing to the cake.

Using Fondant Icing

You can make your own fondant icing (see page 85) or you can buy it ready made at most large supermarkets or specialist food shops. It is quite easy to use:

1. Dust the worktop and your rolling pin well with cornflour.
2. Roll the fondant so that it is about 3mm thick and about the size of the cake you are covering.
3. Lift the fondant on your rolling pin and drape it over the cake. Dip your hands in cornflour, so they aren't sticky, and then press the fondant on to the cake.

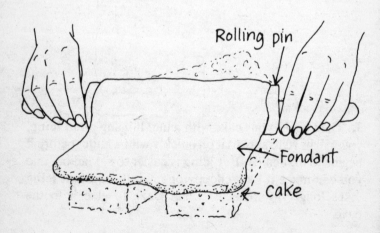

Rolling pin

Fondant

cake

4. Once your cake is covered in icing, the real fun then begins. You can paint designs on the cake with food colouring. Or arrange chocolate drops, small sweets, biscuits, and glacé cherries in patterns and shapes. Cut up liquorice to make numbers, black notes on a piano, eyelashes and brows, tails, wheels, or even a spider's web on a white cake. If you are making a cake house, decorate it with small doll's house furniture and dolls. Cocktail umbrellas or sweet papercases stuck on to cocktail sticks make brollies or lampshades. Scatter hundreds and thousands or desiccated coconut over the surface for a scrunchy texture. You can also use wafers and ice cream cones for funnels and chimneys. In fact, you can use anything you can think of – simply let your imagination run riot!

Clown Face Cake

Serves 8
Time needed 1 hour 15 mins to ice and decorate

You will need

A novelty Victoria sponge (see page 71)
4 tablespoons apricot jam
100g (4oz) fondant icing or white marzipan
Cornflour for rolling
Yellow jelly beans
Smarties
Chocolate drops
Glacé cherries

Chocolate flake
Liquorice
Enough ribbon to go round the cake

Equipment

Rolling pin
Double saucepan or bowl which fits into a saucepan
Sharp knife
Wire rack
Pastry brush
Grater

Instructions

1. Sprinkle cornflour on to a worktop and roll out the marzipan or fondant icing.

2. Fill the saucepan, or the lower saucepan if using a double one, with very hot water. Put the jam into the top saucepan or bowl. Stir until it melts and goes runny.

Double saucepan   Bowl in saucepan

3. Turn the cake upside down and lie it on the icing or

marzipan. Cut round it with a sharp knife. The icing is now exactly the right shape to fit the cake.

4. Turn the cake the right way up and put it on a wire rack.

5. Use the pastry brush to spread the melted apricot jam over the cake.

6. Put the cut-out circle of icing on the cake and press it down gently. The apricot jam will stick it in place.

7. The rest of the ingredients form the clown's face. Stick them on the icing using apricot jam as glue. First grate the chocolate flake and use as a beard.

8. Use the jelly beans as hair.

9. Make glacé cherry eyes.

10. Tie the ribbon round the cake, and glue it under the chin with apricot jam to stop it falling off. Use a bit of sticky tape if you need extra stick.

●●● Christmas Cake

This cake tastes better with the addition of brandy or whisky, but don't forget to ask your parents' permission first before you use it!

Serves about 15 people
Time needed 3½ hours

You will need

250g (10oz) plain flour
1 teaspoon salt
2 teaspoons cinnamon
1 teaspoon grated nutmeg
200g (8oz) butter
200g (8oz) soft brown sugar
4 eggs
1 tablespoon honey
Finely grated zest of 1 lemon and 1 tangerine
120ml (4 fl oz) brandy or whisky
400g (1lb) muscatel raisins
200g (8oz) currants
150g (6oz) glacé cherries
100g (4oz) chopped mixed peel
100g (4oz) walnuts
Plain or fondant icing
A little margarine (for greasing cake tin)

Equipment

Large round or square cake tin
Greaseproof paper (for lining tin)
3 bowls
Sieve
Wooden spoon
Wire rack

Instructions

1. Put the oven on to 150°C/300°F/Gas Mark 2.

2. Grease the cake tin, and line with greaseproof paper (see pictures on page 82).

3. Sift the flour, salt, cinnamon and nutmeg together in the first bowl and put to one side.

4. Cream the butter and sugar in the second bowl until the mixture is light and fluffy.

5. Beat the eggs together and add a little at a time to the creamed fat and sugar, mixing well. Add a tablespoon of the flour with the eggs, as this will help to stop the mixture curdling.

6. Mix the honey, the lemon and tangerine zest, and the brandy or whisky together in a third bowl.

7. Mix the dried fruit and nuts into the flour mixture, as this will stop the fruit sticking together in the cake.

8. Add the flour, fruit and nuts to the butter–sugar mixture in the second bowl, and stir very well.

9. Then add the honey, zest and alcohol mixture to the cake.

10. Stir the mixture well and then spoon it into your greased cake tin.

11. Put it in the oven and bake for 1½ hours. Then reduce the temperature of the oven to 140°C/275°F/Gas Mark 1 and cook for another 3 hours. Check that the top of the cake does not burn during the cooking. Be careful to open the oven door very slowly when you do this, and stand well back, as there will be a rush of hot steam coming out of the oven. Remember to wear gloves or mitts. If the cake starts to look very brown, cover it with a piece of greaseproof paper to stop it browning any more.

12. When the cake has cooked, leave it to cool on a wire rack before decorating with plain or fondant icing (see page 85).

●●● Maria's Chocolate Mayonnaise Cake

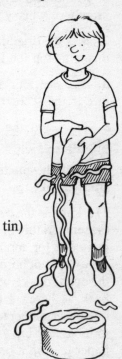

The addition of mayonnaise to this cake makes it lovely and moist. If you like, you can make your own mayonnaise (see page 43), but leave out the mustard and pepper if using the mayonnaise for this recipe.

Serves 8
Time needed 1½ hours

You will need

175g (7oz) mayonnaise
200g (8oz) caster sugar
25g (1oz) cocoa powder
250ml (½pt) water
250g (10oz) self-raising flour
1½ teaspoons baking powder
2 teaspoons vanilla essence
A little margarine (for greasing cake tin)

Icing:

125g (5oz) plain chocolate
50g (2oz) white chocolate

Equipment

20cm (8in) cake tin
Mixing bowl
Balloon whisk or electric food mixer
Bowl

Wire tray

Icing bag and nozzle *or* home–made icing bag, made from greaseproof paper (see diagrams on page 82)

Double saucepan or bowl which fits into a saucepan

Instructions

1. Turn the oven on to 200°C/400°F/Gas Mark 6.

2. Grease the cake tin.

3. Pour the mayonnaise and sugar into a large mixing bowl and whisk until the mixture is light and fluffy.

4. Put the cocoa powder in another bowl and gradually add the water, stirring all the time, until you have a thin cocoa paste.

5. Add the cocoa paste to the sugar and mayonnaise mixture and whisk it in evenly.

6. Mix the flour and baking powder together and add them gradually to the mixture, whisking after each addition. Finally add the vanilla essence and stir into the mixture.

7. Put the mixture in the cake tin and then put this in the oven.

8. Bake for 15 minutes, and then turn the oven down to 150°C/300°F/Gas Mark 2 for half an hour.

9. Take the cake out and stand it on a wire tray to cool.

10. To decorate the cake you will need an icing bag. If you do not have one, you can make one from a sheet of greaseproof paper (see the diagrams on page 82).

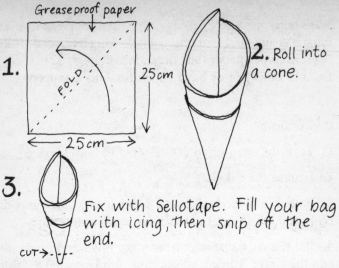

1. Grease proof paper
25cm
25cm
FOLD

2. Roll into a cone.

3. Fix with Sellotape. Fill your bag with icing, then snip off the end.

CUT→

11. Fill the saucepan, or the lower saucepan if using a double one, with very hot water. Break the plain chocolate and put it into the top saucepan or bowl. Stir until the chocolate melts.

12. Pour the melted plain chocolate over the top of the cake and leave it to cool.

13. Melt the white chocolate in the same way you melted the plain chocolate. Pour it into your paper cone. (If you have an icing bag, fit it with a fine nozzle, and pour the chocolate into the bag, then go straight on to instruction 15.)

14. When the cone is full, cut a small hole in the end for the chocolate to be piped out.

15. Holding the bag in the palm of your left hand, and the top of the bag with your right hand, push your thumb down to squeeze out the chocolate. Take it back and forth across the top of the cake to form a stripey pattern. It is important to do this as quickly as possible, before the chocolate begins to set.

●● Clarisse's Yoghurt Cake

This recipe was given to me by a French friend. It is easy to make as all the ingredients are measured
in a yoghurt pot instead of on the scales. You can vary the recipe by adding whatever fruit is in season.

Serves 6
Time needed 1 hour 15 mins

You will need

1 small pot plain yoghurt
2 pots sunflower oil
2 pots caster sugar
4 pots plain flour
1 teaspoon baking powder
4 eggs
1 large cooking apple
A little margarine (for greasing cake tin)

Equipment

20cm (8in) cake tin
2 bowls
Balloon whisk
Sieve
Metal spoon
Sharp knife

Instructions

1. Turn the oven on to 200°C/400°F/Gas Mark 6.

2. Grease the cake tin.

3. Put the yoghurt, oil and sugar in a bowl and whisk together.

4. Sieve the flour and the baking powder into the mixture, and whisk again.

5. Separate the egg yolks from the whites (see page 12) and add the yolks to the cake mix. Whisk until the yolks are mixed in.

6. Whisk the egg whites in a separate bowl until they become stiff and form peaks. Fold into the mixture with a metal spoon.

7. Peel and take out the core of the apple. Chop the apple into small pieces and add them to the cake mix.

8. Place the mixture in the cake tin and put it in the oven. Bake for ¾ hour.

Ideas

Use other fruit, such as bananas, pears or cherries, instead of the apple. You could even use tinned fruit, but *without* the juice or syrup in the tin.

●● Fondant Icing

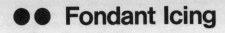

Time needed 30 mins

You will need

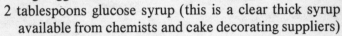

800g (2lb) icing sugar
2 large egg whites
2 tablespoons glucose syrup (this is a clear thick syrup available from chemists and cake decorating suppliers)

Equipment

Sieve
2 bowls
Mixing bowl
Wooden spoon

Instructions

1. Sift the icing sugar into a bowl. Put a small amount of one egg white into a separate bowl in case you need it later. Place the rest of the egg whites and the glucose syrup in a clean, grease-free mixing bowl.

2. Add the icing sugar gradually, and mix with a wooden spoon. As the mixture binds together, knead it with your fingers until it forms a ball. If you find the mixture is too hard add a drop of the egg white you kept in the separate bowl. If it is too soft and runny add some more icing sugar.

3. Sprinkle the work top with icing sugar and knead the icing on the work top until it is pliable (see the diagram on page 86). Store the icing in a plastic bag to prevent it from drying, until you are ready to use it.

● Butter Icing

Time needed 15 mins

You will need

200g (8oz) butter
400g (1lb) icing sugar

Equipment

Mixing bowl
Wooden spoon
Sieve

Instructions

1. Cream the butter in a bowl.

2. Sift the icing sugar a little at a time into the butter. Beat the sugar and butter together until well mixed. Use immediately.

● Plain Icing

Time needed 10 mins

You will need

400g (1lb) icing sugar
Water

Equipment

Sieve
Mixing bowl
Tablespoon
Knife

Instructions

1. Sift the icing sugar into a mixing bowl.

2. Add a tablespoon of water at a time, mixing the icing sugar and water with a knife. Don't put too much water in at once, or the icing will be too runny.

3. Use the icing when it is slightly runny.

Zany Sandwiches

Sandwiches can be a small snack or a complete meal in themselves. Try filling up a pitta with a combination of salad and cheese or meat. Or make a multi-storey sandwich with a variety of different fillings.

Although I have called these recipes sandwich fillings, they can be used on any of the following:

Biscuits and crispbreads
Pitta bread
Rolls
French bread
Crumpets
Muffins
Toast

● Tuna, Mayonnaise, Cheese and Banana

Serves 4
Time needed 15 mins

You will need

175g (7oz) tin of tuna in brine
125g (5oz) cheddar cheese (or any other hard cheese)
200g (8oz) mayonnaise

1 banana
Salt and pepper

Equipment

Tin opener
Bowl
Fork
Grater
Wooden spoon
Sharp knife
Chopping board

Instructions

1. Open the tin of tuna and drain away the brine.

2. Put the tuna in a bowl and flake it with a fork.

3. Grate the cheese and add to the tuna.

4. Mix in the mayonnaise with a wooden spoon.

5. Chop the banana and add it to the mixture.

6. Mash all the ingredients together until they make a lumpy paste. Add salt and pepper to taste.

● Toasted Banana, Cheese and Peanut butter

Serves 1
Time needed 15 mins

You will need

1 slice of bread
Peanut butter
1 banana
Enough cheese to cover the bread in thin slices

Equipment

Knife

Instructions

1. Toast the slice of bread on both sides.

2. Spread on the peanut butter.

3. Slice the banana, and spread this on top of the peanut butter. Then add the cheese slices.

4. Put the bread under the grill for 2 minutes until the cheese is bubbling.

Ideas

If you put your sandwiches in the fridge for an hour before eating them, they will then be firm enough to cut into interesting shapes using pastry cutters.

Here are a few ideas for other combination fillings. I am sure you can think of lots more:

Marmite and toasted cheese
Toasted cheese, salami and mango chutney
Cheese and marmalade
Grated cheese and grated onion
Cream cheese and walnuts

Speedy Sweets

●●● Chewy Fruit and Nut Candies

Time needed 30 mins

You will need

3 heaped tablespoons desiccated coconut
125g (5oz) currants
125g (5oz) seedless raisins
125g (5oz) sultanas
50g (2oz) brazil nuts
50g (2oz) blanched almonds
4 dried apricots

Equipment

Plate
Mincer or liquidizer
Paper cases for sweets

Instructions

1. Tip the coconut on to a plate.

2. Mince all the other ingredients together (this will become very sticky). Or mix them in a liquidizer.

3. Divide the mixture into little balls and roll them in the coconut.

4. Put them into the paper cases and then leave in the fridge until they are firm.

● Coconut Ice

Time needed 4 hours (including setting time)

You will need

1 small tin sweetened condensed milk
225g (9oz) icing sugar
1 teaspoon vanilla essence
150g (6oz) desiccated coconut
Red food colouring

Equipment

2 bowls
Wooden spoon
Shallow rectangular tin (Swiss roll tin)
Knife

Instructions

1. Put the condensed milk, icing sugar and vanilla essence into a bowl.

2. Add the coconut and mix to a stiff dough with a wooden spoon.

3. Divide the mixture into two. Put one half in a second bowl. Add the food colouring to one half of the mixture, and stir it until it turns an even pink colour.

4. Lay the white half of the mixture in the Swiss roll tin. Spread it evenly across the bottom. Put it in the fridge, or freezer if you have one, to harden.

5. Then place the pink half on top of the white and mark the surface into squares with a knife. Put it in the fridge again until it is firm.

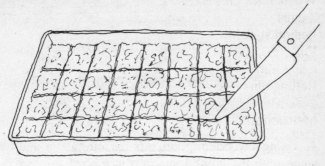

6. When the coconut ice is hard, cut it in small pieces.

●● Marzipan Sweets

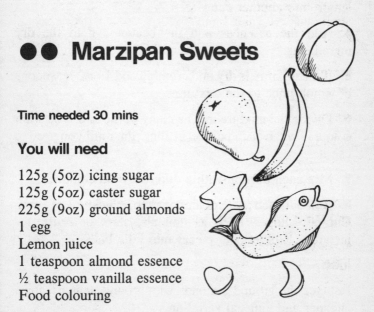

Time needed 30 mins

You will need

125g (5oz) icing sugar
125g (5oz) caster sugar
225g (9oz) ground almonds
1 egg
Lemon juice
1 teaspoon almond essence
½ teaspoon vanilla essence
Food colouring

Equipment

Bowl
Wooden spoon
2 cups
Lemon squeezer
Fork
Cling film
Rolling pin

Instructions

1. Using a wooden spoon, mix the icing sugar and caster sugar with the ground almonds in a bowl.

2. Break the egg into a cup and beat it with a fork.

3. Using the lemon squeezer, squeeze the juice from the lemon into another cup.

4. Add the essences and the beaten egg to the dry ingredients.

5. If the mixture is dry and crumbly add 1 or 2 teaspoons of lemon juice to the mixture.

6. Divide the mixture into as many portions as you want colours. Wrap each portion in cling film until you need to use it.

7. Mix each portion with a different food colouring.

8. Roll out each piece of marzipan to a thickness of 5mm. Cut out shapes, such as animals, stars or fruits, for instance. Roll leftover pieces into little balls.

Idea

Replace the ground almonds with ground peanuts, for a cheaper and unusual variation.

●●● Plain Chocolate Truffles

This recipe needs very hot water, so be careful.

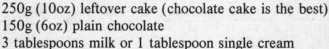

Time needed 30 mins

You will need

250g (10oz) leftover cake (chocolate cake is the best)
150g (6oz) plain chocolate
3 tablespoons milk or 1 tablespoon single cream
1 capful brandy or rum essence (from a small bottle)

Coating:
Cocoa powder *or* dessicated coconut *or* chocolate strands

Equipment

2 small paper or plastic bags
Rolling pin
Double saucepan *or* a bowl which fits into a saucepan
Wooden spoon
Kitchen paper

Instructions

1. Break the cake up into pieces and put these in a bag, sealing the end. Then roll a rolling pin over the bag to crumble the cake pieces.

2. Fill the saucepan, or the lower saucepan if using a double one, with very hot water.

3. Break the chocolate and put it into the top saucepan or bowl. Stir until all the chocolate has melted.

4. Put the cake crumbs into the chocolate mixture and stir with a wooden spoon.

5. Add the cream or milk, and then the brandy or rum essence, and mix in well.

6. Leave the mixture to cool.

7. When the mixture is cold, divide it into tablespoon size pieces and roll into balls in your hands.

8. Put the coating ingredient into a bag and drop the balls in one at a time, and shake them around. The coating will stick to the balls.

9. Place each ball on kitchen paper and leave to harden.

Ideas

Instead of brandy or rum essence, use different essences such as vanilla or orange, or use a teaspoon of coffee mixed with a little water.

Add chopped raisins or nuts to the truffle mixture.

●●● Milk Chocolate Truffles

This recipe needs very hot water so be careful.

Time needed 30 mins

You will need

25g (1oz) butter
125g (5oz) milk chocolate
½ teaspoon vanilla essence
50g (2oz) icing sugar
Cocoa powder and/or desiccated coconut

Equipment

Double saucepan or bowl which fits into a saucepan
Paper cases for sweets

Instructions

1. Fill the saucepan or the lower saucepan if using a double one, with very hot water.

2. Put the butter into the top saucepan or bowl. Break the chocolate and add it to the butter. Stir until melted.

3. Mix the vanilla essence and icing sugar into the chocolate mixture. Leave for 15 minutes until the mixture firms up.

4. Divide the mixture into equal-sized balls.

5. Sprinkle cocoa on one plate and the desiccated

97

coconut on another. Roll the balls in either the cocoa or coconut.

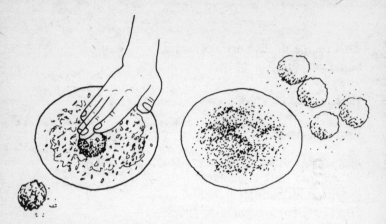

6. Put the truffles in paper cases and leave to harden in the fridge.

Ghost and Ghoul Feast

Why not have a few friends round to tea and make a horror feast!

● Blood and Fingernails Cocktail

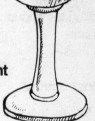

This is a drink served in glasses with 'fingernails' floating on the top!

Serves 8
Time needed 3 mins

You will need

Carton of tomato juice
Some flaked almonds

Equipment

Glasses

Instructions

1. Pour the tomato juice into glasses.

2. Sprinkle a few flaked almonds in the top of each glass.

● Green Slime

This recipe is based on a delicious
Indian drink called *Lassi*, the only
difference being that I have added
green food colouring for a ghoulish effect.

Serves 8
Time needed 5 mins

You will need

120ml (4 fl oz) plain yoghurt
360ml (12 fl oz) ice cold water
1½ tablespoons sugar
1 teaspoon green food colouring

Equipment

Mixing bowl
Wooden spoon
Ladle
Glasses

Instructions

Put all the ingredients in a mixing bowl and mix well
together. Ladle into the glasses to serve.

Ideas

Add less water for a thicker more 'globby' drink.

Add a few grapes to float about in the drink.

● 'Orrible Severed Sandwiches

Serves 8
Time needed 20 mins

You will need

Large loaf of sliced white or brown bread
Butter
Tomato ketchup
2 packets of sliced ham

Equipment

Sharp knife
Chopping board

Instructions

1. Press your hand on to one slice of the bread so that it leaves an impression.

2. Cut round the impression with a sharp knife so that you have a hand shaped piece of bread.

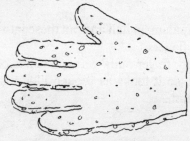

3. Repeat with another slice of bread and butter them both.

4. Rip a slice of ham so that it looks rough at the edges and place it on one of the 'hands' of bread.

5. Spread tomato ketchup on to the 'wrist' and 'fingers' to look like blood.

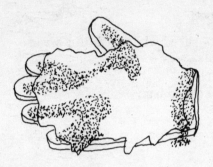

6. Put the other hand-shaped slice of bread on top to complete the sandwich.

7. Repeat the steps to make more 'orrible severed sandwiches.

Ideas

Cut fingers of salami in half and put these into the bread to look like red fingers.
5 Stick almond 'finger nails' on to the ends of the fingers with ketchup, so it looks as though blood is oozing out from underneath.

Ugh!

●● Cucumber Monster

Serves 8
Time needed 30 mins

You will need

1 long cucumber
2 cocktail onions
1 red pepper

Equipment

Sharp knife
Chopping board
Cocktail sticks

Instructions

1. Cut a third off one end of the cucumber and put on one side.

2. Cut a 'V' shape sideways into the other end.

3. Cut several thin 'V' shapes in the top of the cucumber.

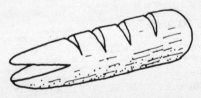

4. Slice the spare third of the cucumber thinly.

5. Insert the slices into the Vs in the back of the cucumber.

6. Pin on two onion eyes with the cocktail sticks.

7. Cut out a tongue from the red pepper and stick it into the mouth with another cocktail stick.

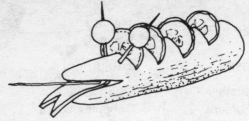

8. You now have a rather nasty–looking cucumber monster!

●● Sugar Mice

The only difficult bit of this recipe is separating the whites of the eggs from the yolks. You must do this properly because if you get yolk into the white it won't whisk properly.

Serves 8
Time needed 30 mins

You will need

2 egg whites
400g (1lb) icing sugar
Peppermint essence
Silver balls
Thin liquorice strips

Equipment

Egg whisk *or* food mixer with a whisk attachment
Sieve
Wooden spoon

Instructions

1. Beat the egg whites until they are stiff, using either an egg whisk or a food mixer with a whisk attachment. A good test to see if the whites are stiff enough is to hold the bowl above your head and see if the mixture moves. If it doesn't, it is stiff enough, but if it does, you'll get egg on your head!

2. Sieve the icing sugar into the egg whites and add a few drops of peppermint essence.

3. Mix well together with a wooden spoon.

4. Form the mixture into mouse shapes.

5. Stick silver balls in for eyes and thin liquorice strips for the tails.

●●● **Spiderweb Cake**

Serves 8
Time needed 30 mins

You will need	Equipment
1 Novelty Victoria sponge (see page 71)	Sieve Bowl

200g (8oz) icing sugar   Tablespoon
Warm water   Knife
1 teaspoon cocoa powder   Piping bag

Instructions

1. Sieve the icing sugar into a bowl. Put 2 tablespoons of the sugar on one side.

2. Mix the rest of the icing sugar with a little warm water. Add the water slowly. The icing mixture should not be too runny.

3. Spoon the icing over the cake and spread it evenly with a knife.

4. Mix the remaining icing sugar with the cocoa powder and a little water, to make chocolate icing.

5. Make a piping bag (see page 82).

6. Pipe a spider web pattern all over the cake with the chocolate icing.

Ideas

Make a marzipan spider (see page 109) to stick on the cake. You could even buy a plastic one together with some plastic flies to decorate the cake. Yuk.

●● Coconut Ghosts

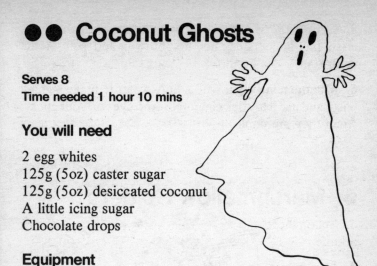

Serves 8
Time needed 1 hour 10 mins

You will need

2 egg whites
125g (5oz) caster sugar
125g (5oz) desiccated coconut
A little icing sugar
Chocolate drops

Equipment

Egg whisk *or* food mixer with whisk attachment
Bowl
Rice paper
Baking tray

Instructions

1. Turn the oven on to 150°C/300°F/Gas Mark 2.

2. Whisk the egg whites until they are stiff and fold in the sugar and coconut.

3. Put the rice paper on a baking tray.

4. Spoon the mixture on to the rice paper in cone shapes.

5. Cook in the oven for about 40 minutes. They should be crisp on the outside, but not brown, and soft in the centre.

6. Mix the icing sugar with a little water to make a gluey paste and use it to stick chocolate drop eyes on your ghosts when they are cool.

● **Marshmallow Spiders**

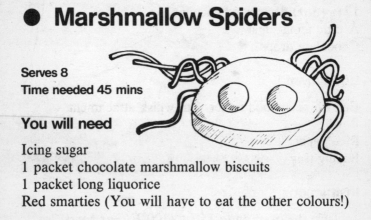

Serves 8
Time needed 45 mins

You will need

Icing sugar
1 packet chocolate marshmallow biscuits
1 packet long liquorice
Red smarties (You will have to eat the other colours!)

Equipment

Bowl
Wooden spoon
Kitchen scissors

Instructions

1. Mix the icing sugar with a little water to make a thick paste.

2. Using the icing sugar as glue, stick two red smartie eyes on to each marshmallow biscuit.

3. Cut long liquorice legs and stick these on to the sides of the marshmallows, again using the icing sugar 'glue'.

●● Marzipan Frogs and Snakes

Make marzipan following the steps on page 93. Then add green food colouring and mix well. Simply mould the marzipan into the shape of frogs and snakes. Stick on chocolate drops for eyes.

●● Monster Faces

Follow the recipes on pages 55 for pizzas, and 57 for baked potatoes, and then decorate them to look like faces. Use jagged strips of ham for teeth, strips of red pepper for a tongue, and mushrooms and tomato slices for eyes.

Presents

● Herb Cheese

Time needed 20 mins

You will need

1 clove of garlic
2–3 tablespoons single
  cream
225g (9oz) cream cheese
3 tablespoons fresh
  mixed herbs

Equipment

Garlic press
Bowl
Wooden spoon
Scissors
Clingfilm

Instructions

1. Peel the garlic and then crush it in a garlic press. Put the crushed garlic in a mixing bowl.

2. Add the cream and cream cheese, and mix well.

3. Using the scissors, cut the herbs very finely into the mixture.

4. Stir it all together and put the herb cheese into tubs.

5. Cover with clingfilm and tie a ribbon around the tubs before giving the herb cheese as a gift.

● Herb Oil

This is very easy present to make
and is a present any cook will
appreciate.

Time needed 5 mins

You will need

Mild-flavoured cooking oil, such as groundnut or
   sunflower seed oil
Fresh herbs – sprigs of rosemary or thyme look very
   pretty

Equipment

A pretty bottle or jar with lid to put the oil in
Funnel

Instructions

1. Pour the oil through the funnel into the bottle, so the
bottle is almost full.

2. Add the herbs to the bottle and screw on the lid.

3. Shake the bottle up and down, so the herbs can be seen floating around.

● **Brandy or Rum Butter**

This tastes delicious eaten with Christmas cake or pudding.

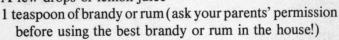

Time needed 20 mins

You will need

50g (2oz) butter
75g (3oz) icing sugar
A few drops of lemon juice
1 teaspoon of brandy or rum (ask your parents' permission
    before using the best brandy or rum in the house!)

Equipment

Bowl
Wooden spoon
Sieve
Clingfilm
Cellophane
Ribbon

Instructions

1. Put the butter in a mixing bowl. Cream it with a

wooden spoon until it is soft.

2. Sieve, then beat the icing sugar into the creamed butter.

3. Add the lemon juice and brandy or rum to the mixture.

4. Mix all the ingredients together well.

5. Put the brandy or rum butter in a decorative pot, cover it with clingfilm and keep it in the fridge.

6. Before giving it as a present, brighten it up with a cellophane and ribbon wrapping.

●● Shortbread

Time needed 1 hour 10 mins

You will need

100g (4oz) plain flour
50g (2oz) ground rice
50g (2oz) caster sugar
Pinch of salt
100g (4oz) butter (soft)

Equipment

Bowl
Sieve
Greaseproof paper
Baking tray
Fork
Knife
Wire rack

Instructions

1. Turn the oven on to 180°C/350°F/Gas Mark 4.

2. In a mixing bowl, sieve together the flour, ground rice, caster sugar and salt.

3. Rub in the butter with your fingertips, lifting it while you rub to aerate the mixture. The dough should be the consistency of shortcrust pastry.

4. Knead the dough to a ball and then put it on a piece of greaseproof paper and very gently press and roll it to a round about 1 cm thick.

5. Lift the paper with the shortbread on to a baking tray.

6. Prick the shortbread all over with a fork and mark sections and a pretty edge with a knife.

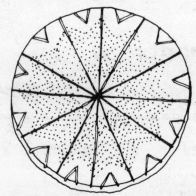

7. Bake in the oven for about 45 minutes. The shortbread should be firm to touch and a light golden colour.

8. Put it on a wire rack to cool. When cold, cut the shortbread into the marked triangles.

Ideas

Add 50g (2oz) chopped walnuts *or* 50g (2oz) chopped cherries to the shortbread mixture for a special occasion.

●● Gingerbread Men and Women

Serves 6
Time needed 40 mins

You will need

250g (10oz) self-raising flour
1 tablespoon ground ginger
75g (3oz) margarine or butter
125g (5oz) golden syrup
125g (5oz) brown sugar
2 tablespoonfuls milk
Plain flour (for flouring work top)
A little margarine (for greasing baking tray)

To decorate:

Tube of ready-made icing

Equipment

Sieve
Large bowl
Wooden spoon
Rolling pin
Baking tray
Gingerbread men and women cutters

Instructions

1. Turn the oven on to 180°C/350°F/Gas Mark 4.

115

2. Sift the flour and ground ginger into the bowl. Add the margarine or butter and rub in finely using only your fingertips.

3. Mix the syrup, sugar and milk together, and add to the other ingredients. Mix with a wooden spoon to form a dough.

4. Lightly flour a work top and roll out the dough so it is about 5mm thick all over.

5. Put the dough in the fridge for half an hour to harden, before cutting out your gingerbread people.

6. Grease a baking tray.

7. Take the dough out of the fridge, and cut out gingerbread people using the cutters. Place the figures on the baking tray, leaving gaps between them so the dough can spread.

8. Bake in the oven for about 15 minutes, or until the gingerbread figures are golden brown.

9. Put them on a wire tray to cool.

10. When cool, decorate with the tube of icing, making buttons, stripes and faces.

11. If you are giving the gingerbread figures as a present, stack them carefully in a tin so they won't break.

Food Jewellery

You can make jewellery from sweets, nuts, raisins, pasta, and even popcorn. Give it a coat of clear varnish – nail varnish will do – for a shiny sparkle, or simply keep it as it is and eat it when you are hungry!

● Simple Sweet Necklace

Time needed 10 mins

You will need

Mints or boiled sweets with holes at their centres
Plastic or embroidery thread

Instructions

Cut a piece of thread about 15cm long. Then thread the sweets on to it and tie the ends together.

117

●● Another Sweet Necklace

Time needed 30 mins

You will need

Shirring elastic (this comes in reels like cotton thread)
1 blunt needle (an embroidery needle will do)
1 packet miniature sweets, such as jelly tots, liquorice
    allsorts, or candy tots
Damp cloth
Clear nail varnish

Instructions

1. Cut a piece of shirring elastic about 15 cm long and tie a knot at one end.

2. Thread the elastic through the needle. Now thread the sweets on to the elastic, by pushing the needle through them, one at a time. The needle is likely to become very sticky with the sugary coating on the sweets, so you will need to wipe it occasionally with the damp cloth.

4. If you don't want to eat the sweets once they are threaded on the necklace, give them a coat of clear nail varnish.

Idea

For a healthier edible necklace, thread raisins or popcorn on to the elastic.

● Pasta Wheel Bracelet

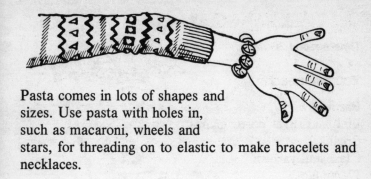

Pasta comes in lots of shapes and
sizes. Use pasta with holes in,
such as macaroni, wheels and
stars, for threading on to elastic to make bracelets and
necklaces.

Time needed 40 mins

You will need

Poster paint
Paint brush
36 pasta wheels

Instructions

1. Using a fine paint brush and different coloured poster
paints, paint the pasta wheels around their edges and leave
to dry.

2. Thread the wheels on to shirring elastic and then tie the
ends together.

● Pasta Bow Brooch

Time needed 30 mins

You will need

Pasta bow
Pink and silver poster paints
Brush
Clear nail varnish
PVA glue
A brooch back

Instructions

1. Paint the pasta bow with pink poster paint and leave it to dry.

2. Paint dots on with silver paint, and leave to dry again.

3. Then varnish the bow with clear nail varnish.

4. When the varnish is dry, turn the brooch over and stick on the brooch back with PVA glue. Leave it to dry.

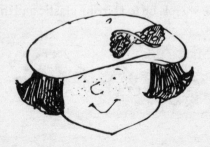

Odds and Ends

● Homemade Breadcrumbs

These are useful for coating fish,
chicken pies and Scotch eggs for
example.

Time needed 25 mins

You will need

Some bits of leftover ends and crusts of bread (make sure
that none is mouldy)

Equipment

Baking tray
Polythene bag
Rolling pin
Jar and lid

Instructions

1. Put the oven on to a low temperature, about 150°C/
300°F/Gas Mark 2. Place the pieces of bread on a baking
tray, and put this in the oven.

2. Leave the tray in the oven for 20 minutes, until the
bread is completely dry and pale brown.

3. Then put the bread into a polythene bag, seal the end, and roll a rolling pin over the bag, crushing the bread into crumbs.

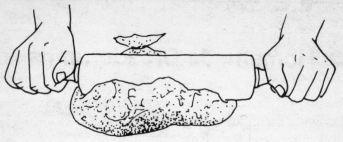

4. Store the breadcrumbs in an airtight jar.

● Muesli

The Swiss invented muesli for breakfast. It can be full of many different kinds of fruits, nuts and cereals, and you can eat it with fruit juice, milk, cream or yoghurt.

Serves 6
Time needed 15 mins

You will need

200g (8oz) porridge oats
4 tablespoons sultanas
50g (2oz) desiccated coconut
50g (2oz) chopped brazil nuts
50g (2oz) chopped dates
50g (2oz) dried banana

Equipment

Bowl
Wooden spoon
Jar and lid

Instructions

Put all the ingredients in a mixing bowl, and mix well together. Store in an airtight jar.

To serve:

Serve with one of the following: milk, fruit juice, yoghurt or cream.

●●● White Sauce

Sauce making is not difficult as long as you take your time and follow the instructions carefully.
You can make lots of different sauces using the same basic method and adding different flavourings. The method given below is known as the roux method.

Makes 250ml (½pt)
Time needed 20 mins

You will need

25g (1oz) butter or
    margarine

Equipment

Saucepan
Metal spoon

25g (1oz) plain flour
250ml (½pt) milk
Salt and pepper *and* flavourings (see Ideas)

Instructions

1. Melt the butter in a heavy saucepan, stir in the flour and continue stirring over a low heat for 1–2 minutes, using a metal spoon.

2. Remove the pan from the heat, and *gradually* stir in half the milk and beat it until it is smooth. If the liquid is added too quickly *or* you stir it too slowly, lumps will form!

3. When the uncooked sauce is quite smooth, return the pan to the heat. Stirring vigorously all the time, bring the sauce slowly to boiling point. Again lumps may form if the sauce is heated too quickly or you stir too slowly.

4. Add the remaining milk and stir well. Bring the sauce back to the boil and simmer for 2 minutes, stirring constantly.

5. Add salt and pepper, and other flavourings if you like. The Ideas section gives some suggestions:

Ideas
Cheese sauce:

Add 100g (4oz) grated cheese to the basic sauce, and use it with macaroni to make macaroni cheese. Or, use it with a bolognaise sauce and pre-cooked lasagna to make lasagna. Be careful not to let the sauce burn once you have added the cheese.

Parsley sauce:

Add 1 tablespoon of finely chopped parsley, and serve

with fish and new potatoes.

Onion sauce:

Add 1 chopped boiled onion, and serve with ham.

Egg sauce:

Add 1 chopped hard-boiled egg and serve with meat or fish.

Pastry Making

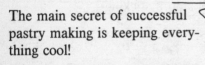

The main secret of successful pastry making is keeping everything cool!

1. Fat should be kept in the fridge until ready to use.

2. Water should be fresh from the cold tap.

3. Your hands should be clean and cold.

4. Handle the pastry as little as possible and only with your fingertips.

5. Make sure you use plain flour.

6. The best fats for pastry making are a mixture of lard and butter or margarine.

7. Use the correct proportions of fat to flour. If you use too much flour you will make tough pastry. Too much fat will make the pastry difficult to mix. Too much water will make the pastry sticky to handle and tough when cooked.

Too little water produces pastry that is too 'short' and crumbly.

8. Knead the pastry only just enough to mix it smoothly. If you handle it too much it will become tough.

9. Allow the pastry to stand in a cool place before cooking.

10. Bake pastry in a fairly hot oven. Too cool an oven allows the fat to melt and run out of the pastry before it can be absorbed. Too great a heat hardens the pastry before it has risen.

11. Reduce the heat of the oven once the pastry has turned golden brown.

12. Do not grease the baking tin before cooking pastry, as the fat in the pastry will stop it sticking.

13. The general proportions for pastry making are these:

½ fat to flour
1 teaspoon of salt to each pound of flour
4–5 tablespoons of water to each pound of flour.

● Basic Short Crust Pastry

Serves 8
Time needed 35 mins

You will need

500g (1lb 4oz) plain flour

½ level teaspoon salt
250g (10oz) fat (made up of 125g (5oz) lard and
    125g (5oz) butter)
8–10 tablespoons water

Equipment

Sieve
Large mixing bowl
Knife
Palate knife
Rolling pin

Instructions

1. Sieve the flour with the salt into the bowl.

2. Cut the fat into thin pieces using a knife, and drop it into the bowl.

3. Rub the fat into the flour using only your fingertips. Keep your hands above the bowl to aerate the flour. When the mixture looks like fine breadcrumbs, stop rubbing.

4. Pour the water into the mixture and stir with a palate knife.

5. Pull the pastry together into a ball and knead it into the shape required.

6. Roll it out on a table or board dusted with flour.

7. Allow the pastry to stand in a cool place for 15 minutes before working.

Acknowledgements

Special thanks to Ann-Marie Mulligan who tested every recipe in this book and remained cheerful throughout!

Kenwood for the loan of the Kenwood chef and attachments.

Kitchens of Whiteladies Road, Bristol, and Quiet Street, Bath, for the cake moulds.

Useful Reference Books

Cooking Explained by Barbara Hammond, revised by Jill Davies, published by Longmans.

Diet and Nutrition by Dr Gordon Jackson, published by Salamander.